YALE LAW LIBRARY SERIES IN LEGAL HISTORY AND REFERENCE